A
MASTER
ENGINEER

Macdonald

Contents

Introduction   5

Plans for a Journey   6

Paddington Station   8

On the Train   11

The Great Western Railway   12

A Visit to a Workshed   14

The Trade Fair   16

Down at the Docks   18

Lost!   21

The Chocolate Factory   22

Crossing the Avon   24

A Royal Occasion   26

Picture Glossary   28

Finding Out More   30

Introduction

This book tells the story of Henry, who lived in London during the reign of Queen Victoria. In the summer of 1859, he and his father set off on a long journey by rail, to visit an engineering trade fair in Bristol and to attend the grand opening ceremony of the Royal Albert Bridge in Cornwall. Henry's father was an engineer. He owned several ironworks, where essential parts for the bridge, such as cast-iron nuts and bolts, had been made. He took Henry with him on this trip so that his son could learn more about engineering, and see how the objects made by his father's business were put to use.

In 1859 railway travel was still quite new and exciting. The Great Western Railway line to Bristol, which Henry and his father travelled on, had been opened in 1841. It had been designed by the great engineer, Isambard Kingdom Brunel, who also designed the Royal Albert Bridge, and many other famous buildings. Henry's father admired Brunel's skill and energy very much. Like Brunel, he too was full of schemes and grand ideas for future projects, although his plans were always concerned with his own business ventures, and how to make them more profitable!

Henry and his family were rich. They lived in a warm, comfortable house with servants to look after them. Not everyone in Victorian England enjoyed the same high standard of living. In Bristol, Henry met Tom, a boy of his own age, who had to work as an errand boy to help his mother pay for food and lodgings for the rest of their family. Down by the docks, he saw slum housing, and beggars. But Henry also saw how some factory owners tried to improve conditions for their workers, by providing better housing, or free lessons.

Some of the inventions and projects designed by Victorian engineers are illustrated at the end of this book. In addition there are suggestions for places to visit and books to read.

Plans for a Journey

'Haven't you finished your porridge yet, Henry?' asked Mama. 'Come on now, eat up! You're keeping the servants waiting. They want to clear the table and wash up our breakfast dishes.' She turned to her husband. 'Don't go filling Henry's head with wild ideas about new engineering projects. He's got a lot to learn at school before he can join you at the ironworks.'

Henry's father looked up from the map he was studying. 'Mmm, yes, dear,' he said vaguely.

Mama sighed. 'I sometimes wonder why I bother,' she said, but she didn't seem too cross.

'So you see, Henry,' said Papa, 'if we caught the train, we could visit the big trade fair at Bristol on our way to Cornwall. I've got to be at the opening ceremony of the new bridge they've been building down there, because our firm has supplied some of the parts. It would take days by coach and horses, and we wouldn't have time to go to Bristol as well. It would be so much quicker by the railway.'

Alice and Matilda, Henry's sisters, protested. 'It's not fair!' they shouted. 'Why can't we come too? Henry has already been on a train. We haven't. Henry always goes on trips with Papa. It's our turn!'

'Girls, girls, less noise please!' said Mama. 'You might not like travelling by train. People tell me that it's noisy and dirty, and that doesn't sound very pleasant. And you know that Henry travels with Papa so that he can learn about engineering. He will have to take over the business when Papa grows old, after all.' She smiled at the two girls, who still looked rather disgruntled. 'But who knows, perhaps we might all go on a railway excursion one day in the summer. Perhaps we could go to one of the new seaside towns, like Brighton or Hastings.'

Papa got up from the table. 'It's time I was at work,' he said. 'There's a lot to see to before we set off for Cornwall. Now, girls, off you go to the schoolroom. Your governess will be waiting. And you, Henry, listen carefully to what the masters have to say to you at school. If you want to be a good engineer, you'll have to study hard!'

Paddington Station

Henry and Papa were at Paddington Station, waiting to catch the train to Bristol. The huge station was packed with travellers and their luggage. Great locomotives hissed and roared as stokers shovelled coal into the fireboxes. The coals glowed red hot and heated the water in the locomotive boilers until it turned into steam.

'And it's the steam,' explained Papa, 'that drives the engines along. The stokers have to make sure that the fires keep burning throughout the journey, so that the locomotives can keep up speed. These new trains can travel at 60 miles per hour on the Bristol run. It used to take days by coach and horses and it was *so* uncomfortable.'

'It's hard work being a stoker,' thought Henry. 'I'd much rather be an engine driver. Better still, I'd like to design the fastest engine ever!'

His thoughts were interrupted by a nervous voice at his side.

'Now just hold on tight to my hand, Henry,' said Aunt Charlotte. 'I don't like crowds like this. You never know who's going to be standing next to you.

There are probably thieves and pickpockets and even murderers here. And it's such a crush! I feel quite faint with all the heat and the noise . . . and the smells are dreadful! Ooh! What was that?!' Aunt Charlotte gave a jump of fright. One of the great locomotives had let out a sudden hiss of steam.

Henry and his father had agreed to accompany Aunt Charlotte as far as Reading, where she wanted to visit some friends. She had never travelled by train before and was rather scared of the journey.

'But now that dear Queen Victoria has travelled by the railway, we ought to follow her brave example,' said Aunt Charlotte. 'But I must say, I don't feel very brave.'

'Don't worry, Aunt,' said Henry. 'It's quite safe. And the carriages are very comfortable inside. Just wait and see.'

'All aboard! All aboard!' A porter in a smart green uniform yelled out the names of stations. 'Hurry along now! All passengers for the Great Western Railway service to Reading, Swindon and Bristol!'

'That's our train,' said Papa excitedly. 'Come on!'

On the Train

'I must say, Henry,' said Aunt Charlotte, 'you were right about the carriages being comfortable. It's all very nice in here. Look, there are padded head-rests, and arm-rests between the seats.'

'And it's properly heated,' said Papa. 'In the very early days of the railway, we were half-frozen in winter. And now they've put in proper luggage racks, too. This carriage has even got special places to hang top-hats. It's the first time I've seen that!'

They had found three seats in a first-class carriage. Henry managed to get a seat next to the window, so he felt very pleased. He wanted to see everything on this journey. For the moment, he amused himself by looking at the other passengers in the carriage. He tried to guess what reasons they could have for their journeys. A handsome soldier and his young wife sat opposite him. They told him that they were travelling home after three years in India. In the far corner of the carriage sat an old man reading a newspaper. Henry was surprised to see that the paper was printed in French, but then he remembered that Papa had said that people came from all over Europe to visit the trade fairs. There was also a rather shy young girl, sitting quietly beside her governess. He found out that they, too, were visiting friends in Reading.

His aunt's voice interrupted his thoughts. 'Just think,' she was saying to Papa, 'how many changes there have been since you and I were young! In those days, travel took so long, and the roads were often very bad. Now people can travel so fast and easily all over the country, sometimes just for pleasure.'

'And it's not just people,' replied Papa. 'Railways are used now to carry animals to market and all sorts of goods to the towns. They also carry raw materials like coals and iron ore from the mines to the factories. We use the railways to transport the heavy castings that we make in our ironworks, too. Now we sell our goods all over the country, even as far south as this new bridge in Cornwall.'

He laughed. 'We engineers invented railways. Who knows what other wonderful machines we can invent?'

The Great Western Railway

Henry munched the last few mouthfuls of biscuit and brushed the crumbs from his knees. 'They're good,' he said approvingly. 'Do you have any of yours left over, Aunt Charlotte?'

The biscuits were a free sample. All the first-class passengers had found a packet on their seat. Henry read the printed wrapper. 'Messrs Huntley and Palmers Biscuit Manufactory, Reading.'

'That's right,' said Papa. 'You'll be able to see their factory from the train. It's not long before we get there. Do you have your luggage ready, Charlotte?'

The train stopped at Reading Station and Aunt Charlotte got out carefully. Her friends were waiting to meet her. Henry waved goodbye.

'Look at the station, Henry,' said Papa. 'It's one of the best on the Great Western Line. All the platforms are under cover so passengers don't get cold and wet while they're waiting for the trains.'

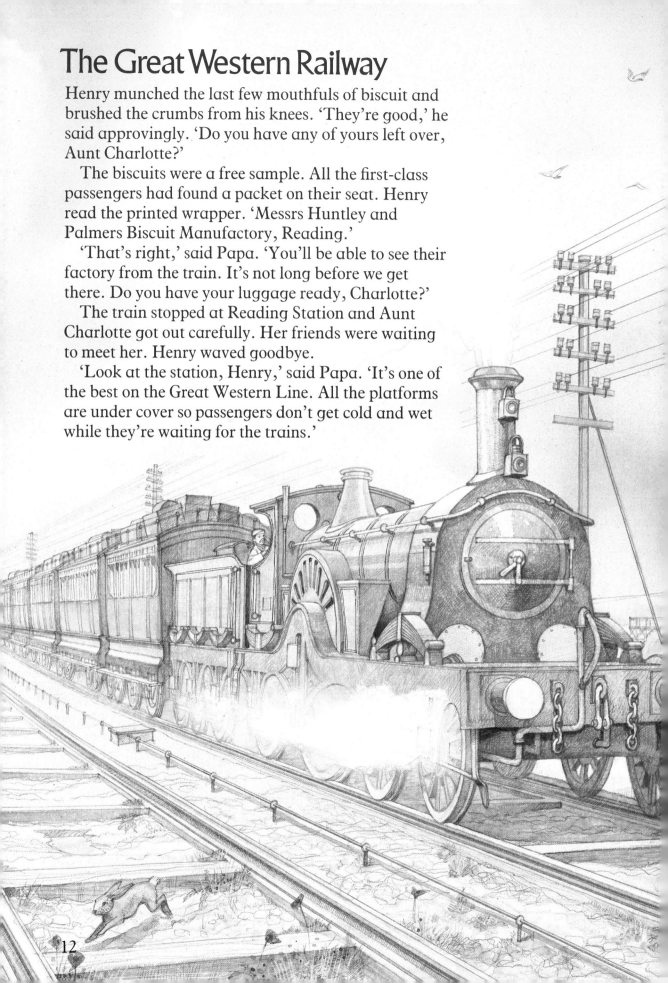

Slowly, with clouds of smoke and a great shower of sparks, the locomotive pulled the train out of the station. Henry looked out of the window.

'There's a canal down there,' he said. 'I can see a narrowboat going under the bridge. Did you really send all your cast iron by canal before the railways were built, Papa?'

'We did,' said Papa. 'And I can remember how excited we were when plans were drawn up for the new railway lines. We saw how they could help our business. But it was hard work building the railways. They had to dig tunnels and blast cuttings through solid rock. They say it took thousands of men six whole years to build this line. And I'm afraid that many men died in the process. Some were killed by rock falls or in accidents with gunpowder. Others died when tunnels collapsed, or from diseases brought on by exhaustion. Brunel designed this line. He may be a great engineer, but his foremen were hard taskmasters!'

Papa turned to look out of the window. 'Look, there are the wires for the telegraph signalling system,' he said. 'The Great Western was one of the first companies to install them. They can send messages along the wires to every station down the line.'

13

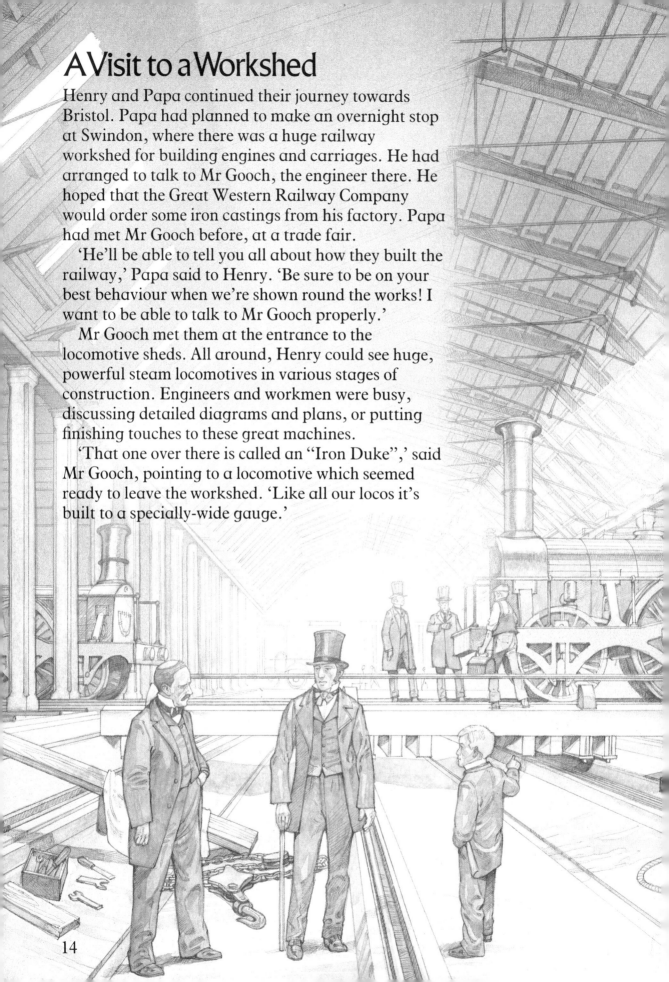

A Visit to a Workshed

Henry and Papa continued their journey towards Bristol. Papa had planned to make an overnight stop at Swindon, where there was a huge railway workshed for building engines and carriages. He had arranged to talk to Mr Gooch, the engineer there. He hoped that the Great Western Railway Company would order some iron castings from his factory. Papa had met Mr Gooch before, at a trade fair.

'He'll be able to tell you all about how they built the railway,' Papa said to Henry. 'Be sure to be on your best behaviour when we're shown round the works! I want to be able to talk to Mr Gooch properly.'

Mr Gooch met them at the entrance to the locomotive sheds. All around, Henry could see huge, powerful steam locomotives in various stages of construction. Engineers and workmen were busy, discussing detailed diagrams and plans, or putting finishing touches to these great machines.

'That one over there is called an "Iron Duke",' said Mr Gooch, pointing to a locomotive which seemed ready to leave the workshed. 'Like all our locos it's built to a specially-wide gauge.'

'What does that mean?' asked Henry, puzzled.

'It means that its wheels are farther apart than the wheels on locomotives used by other railway companies,' replied Mr Gooch. 'Our company chairman, Mr Brunel – he's the famous engineer who designed this railway, you know – thinks that a wider gauge makes travel safer and more comfortable. But it means, of course, that our locomotives can only run on our own railway lines, which have been specially built to fit. Mr Brunel believes that, in time, all the other companies will come round to his way of thinking, and change over to the wide gauge.'

'I'm not so sure of that myself,' said Papa. 'But now, Mr Gooch, let's talk business. Tell me about those bolts you need for repairing the boilers.'

On their way back to the station, Henry and Papa passed rows and rows of neat, new, box-like houses.

'Those are company houses, where the railway workmen live,' explained Papa. 'Before they built the workshops, Swindon was a sleepy little market town. Now look at it!'

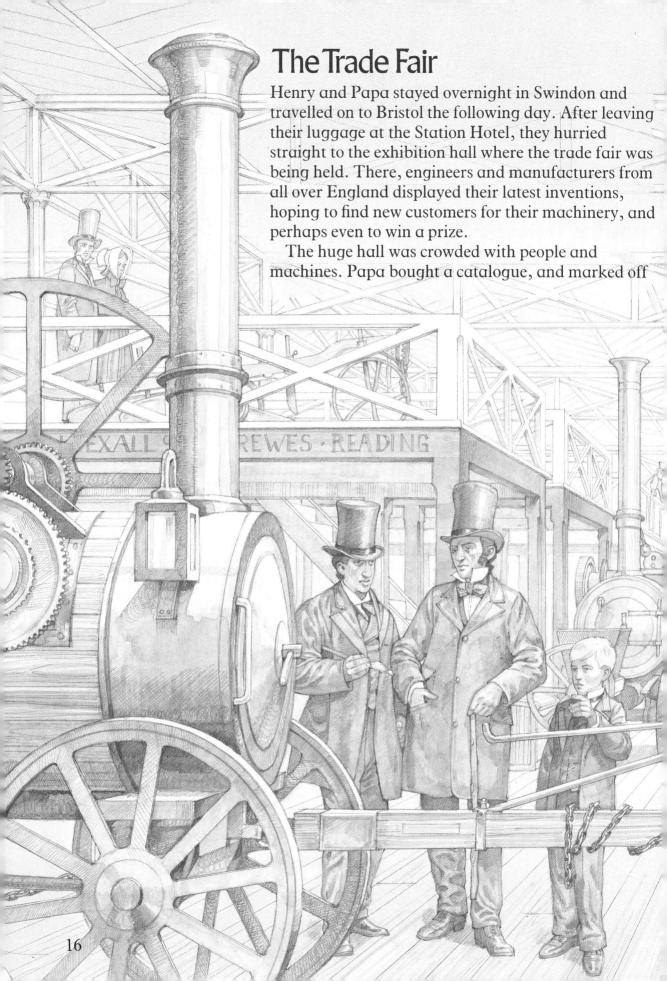

The Trade Fair

Henry and Papa stayed overnight in Swindon and travelled on to Bristol the following day. After leaving their luggage at the Station Hotel, they hurried straight to the exhibition hall where the trade fair was being held. There, engineers and manufacturers from all over England displayed their latest inventions, hoping to find new customers for their machinery, and perhaps even to win a prize.

The huge hall was crowded with people and machines. Papa bought a catalogue, and marked off

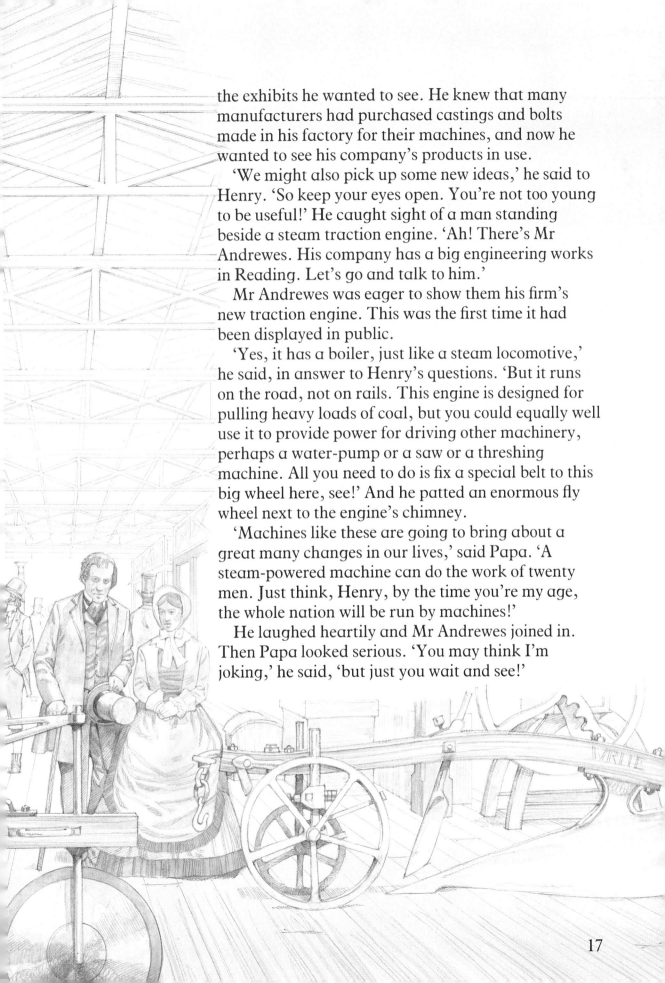

the exhibits he wanted to see. He knew that many manufacturers had purchased castings and bolts made in his factory for their machines, and now he wanted to see his company's products in use.

'We might also pick up some new ideas,' he said to Henry. 'So keep your eyes open. You're not too young to be useful!' He caught sight of a man standing beside a steam traction engine. 'Ah! There's Mr Andrewes. His company has a big engineering works in Reading. Let's go and talk to him.'

Mr Andrewes was eager to show them his firm's new traction engine. This was the first time it had been displayed in public.

'Yes, it has a boiler, just like a steam locomotive,' he said, in answer to Henry's questions. 'But it runs on the road, not on rails. This engine is designed for pulling heavy loads of coal, but you could equally well use it to provide power for driving other machinery, perhaps a water-pump or a saw or a threshing machine. All you need to do is fix a special belt to this big wheel here, see!' And he patted an enormous fly wheel next to the engine's chimney.

'Machines like these are going to bring about a great many changes in our lives,' said Papa. 'A steam-powered machine can do the work of twenty men. Just think, Henry, by the time you're my age, the whole nation will be run by machines!'

He laughed heartily and Mr Andrewes joined in. Then Papa looked serious. 'You may think I'm joking,' he said, 'but just you wait and see!'

Down at the Docks

'Let's take a walk before we go back to the hotel,' said Papa. 'I could do with some fresh air after that exhibition hall. It was so stuffy in there! Would you like to see the docks?'

'Yes, that would be great!' replied Henry. 'Which way do we go?'

Arriving at the dockyards was like entering another world. Exotic, enticing smells from sacks of tropical fruit and coffee beans mingled with the rich odours of wine and spices and the salty breeze from the sea. Choking, tarry smoke from the shipyards drifted everywhere. Seagulls mewed and screamed overhead, watching out for tasty morsels thrown overboard. Rats scuttled away to hide in corners or under tarpaulins. Mangy cats slunk noiselessly past, hunting them. Henry peered down dingy alleyways and into ramshackle courtyards between the warehouses. He thought he saw a sailor with an eyepatch and gold earrings. Could he be a pirate? They met an old woman begging. Papa gave her a

18

penny. As they walked past a busy tavern, Henry listened to snatches of song, and voices shouting in languages he had never heard before. Two drunken sailors staggered out of one alehouse, supported by several giggling young women.

Papa shook his head. 'Drunkenness is a terrible vice. Be warned, Henry!'

On the quayside, they were able to get quite close to some of the ships. Henry watched a cargo of cocoa beans being unloaded from a sailing ship. They had been transported thousands of miles from Africa. On the opposite side of the harbour, Papa pointed out the works of one of Bristol's best-known shipbuilders.

'Look, there's Stothert and Marten's shipyard,' he said. 'And there's their famous paddle steamer, the *Taff*. It's the fastest steamship on the Bristol Channel. Its engines can produce 100 horsepower. That's almost as much as a locomotive. The company is building lots more like her. Soon, steamships will replace the old sailing vessels, like this one in front of us. Now, there's another new opportunity to expand our business!'

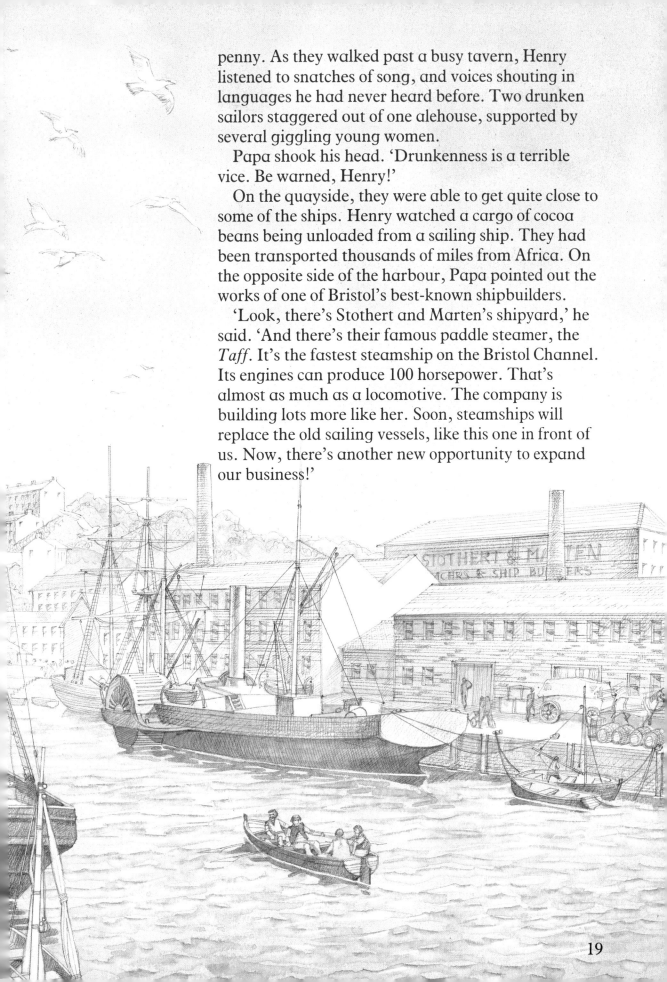

Lost!

The following morning, Henry and Papa set out again for the trade fair. Papa had lots of exhibits he still wanted to see. After a while, Henry became bored. Papa spent so long looking at each machine!

'I wonder if Papa would notice if I went out and explored a bit,' thought Henry. 'He's so busy, I'm sure I could slip out for half an hour or so and be back before he realised I was gone.'

So, he left Papa deep in conversation with a man demonstrating a new type of steam engine, and made his way out of the hall.

He set off briskly along the route he had taken yesterday with Papa, but soon he realised that he was walking along streets he did not recognise. Somewhere, he must have taken a wrong turning. He tried to retrace his steps, but that didn't seem to help. He walked on, and found himself in a crowded, dirty street where some sort of market was taking place. Loud-voiced men shouted the prices of the goods they were trying to sell. Ragged women and girls trudged past with baskets of fruit and trays of limp flowers. There was mud and dirt and smelly rubbish everywhere. The noise was deafening.

Suddenly, Henry fell heavily to the ground. He had slipped on some half-rotten cabbage leaves. He sat there for a moment, trying to get his breath back and wondering what to do next. He was totally lost and in a strange city.

A voice behind him made him jump. He looked up, and saw a boy of his own age, dressed in neat but very patched and threadbare clothes. 'Are you all right, mate? No bones broken?'

Henry got up, rather stiffly. 'No, I'm not hurt,' he said, 'but thank you for asking.'

'You don't come from round here,' said the boy. 'You don't speak like us. Stranger, are you?'

Henry couldn't decide whether the boy was being friendly or not. 'Yes, that's right,' he said. He hoped he didn't sound nervous. 'I'm from London. My father's visiting the trade fair. I came with him.'

'Well, where is he?' said the boy. 'Or have you gone and lost him?'

The Chocolate Factory

Henry explained what had happened.

'Well,' said the boy, whose name was Tom, 'you'd better come with me. I'm on my way home from work. I've got to collect my Ma's dinner and take it to her at the factory. My sister will have cooked it by now. She's a really good cook.'

'What!' said Henry. 'Don't you go to school? And why do you and your mother work? Why is your sister keeping house for you? Where's your father? What does he do?'

'Hold on a minute!' said Tom. 'One question at a time! Are they all as nosey as you in London? If you really want to know, my father is a sailor. He's away at sea for months at a time. Sometimes he brings

home lots of money, but sometimes the money runs out before he can get back. I work as a message boy, and Ma works in the factory to feed us and pay for our lodgings. My oldest sister is ten and she keeps house, like I said, and looks after the two little ones. I'd like to go to school, because learning helps you get on in life, but we need the money I earn. Maybe, if I get a job at the factory, I can go to the night school the bosses run there for the workers. But come on now, or I'll be late.'

Tom's mother worked in Fry's chocolate factory. Henry could smell it long before they reached the gates. It made him feel quite sick.

'You don't notice the smell once you've worked there for some time,' said Tom.

He led the way past huge storerooms and machine rooms to the mixing room where his mother worked. Henry was fascinated to see the huge vats where cocoa, extracted from crushed cocoa beans, was mixed with sugar and milk before being shaped into chocolate bars. Tom introduced Henry to his mother and explained how they had met.

'Well, Henry, it's nice to make your acquaintance,' said Tom's mother. 'Tom doesn't often bring me visitors! Now, Tom, stay out of the way of those machines while I eat my pie. You'd better show Henry how to find his way back to the exhibition hall. His father will be worried to death by now.'

23

Crossing the Avon

Tom took Henry to the exhibition organiser's office, and soon Papa came rushing in.

'I owe you a great many thanks, young man,' Papa said to Tom. 'I thought we'd lost this silly boy for good! Now Tom, where does your mother live? I must call on her to thank her for her good sense and to congratulate her on having such a kind boy. You, Henry, will wait in the hotel until I get back.'

Henry sat in the hotel room, wondering what his father would say to him when he got back. Eventually, he heard his father's heavy footsteps.

'Now for a real telling off,' he thought, gloomily. But, to his surprise, all his father said was 'Get your coat and hat. We're going out.' He was even more surprised to see Tom waiting in the hotel lobby. All three of them got into a horse-drawn cab.

'We're going to the rope bridge,' explained Papa. 'It's one of the great sights of Bristol. Tom deserves a treat as a reward for finding you!'

Papa went on, 'I'd like to see the bridge, too. It was designed by the great engineer, Brunel, at the start of his career. He ran out of money, and wasn't able to finish it, but it's still pretty impressive, eh, Tom?'

They all agreed. Even in its unfinished state, the bridge was spectacular. Brunel had chosen to build it where the River Avon ran between high stone cliffs. There was a partly-built tower on either side of the river, with a slender iron bar stretching between them.

'Brunel had to stop when he got this far,' said Papa, 'but he'll finish it some day, when there's enough money! It costs a penny each to cross. Shall we go?'

'Yes, please, sir!' replied Tom, excitedly.

'But how?' said Henry. 'You can't cross that!'

Then he saw a small basket, fixed to the iron bar with ropes and pulleys, moving jerkily between the towers. There were four people in it.

'You see,' said Papa. 'You cross the river in that basket. Come along! We must climb the tower to get to the landing platform. This is one of the wonders of engineering, my lad. We mustn't miss out on it!'

A Royal Occasion

It was time to start on the final leg of their journey –
the opening of the bridge in Cornwall. Henry and
Papa left Bristol by a Great Western Railway train
and arrived at Plymouth several hours later. Then
they set off for the Royal opening ceremony at
Saltash, where the new bridge was. Henry soon
caught sight of it, crossing the River Tamar which
divides the counties of Devon and Cornwall.

'The new bridge means that the railways can
progress into Cornwall at last,' said Papa. 'Until now,
the trains have always had to stop at the river.' He
looked at his newspaper. 'According to this, it's a very
wide river. It says here that the bridge is over 700
metres long and stands 30 metres above the water.

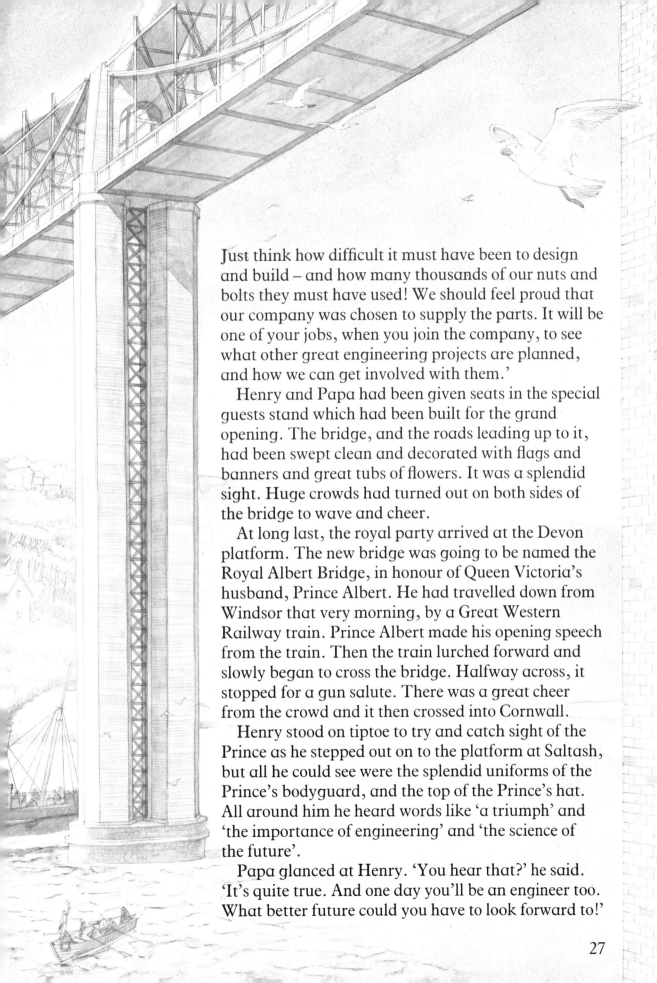

Just think how difficult it must have been to design and build – and how many thousands of our nuts and bolts they must have used! We should feel proud that our company was chosen to supply the parts. It will be one of your jobs, when you join the company, to see what other great engineering projects are planned, and how we can get involved with them.'

Henry and Papa had been given seats in the special guests stand which had been built for the grand opening. The bridge, and the roads leading up to it, had been swept clean and decorated with flags and banners and great tubs of flowers. It was a splendid sight. Huge crowds had turned out on both sides of the bridge to wave and cheer.

At long last, the royal party arrived at the Devon platform. The new bridge was going to be named the Royal Albert Bridge, in honour of Queen Victoria's husband, Prince Albert. He had travelled down from Windsor that very morning, by a Great Western Railway train. Prince Albert made his opening speech from the train. Then the train lurched forward and slowly began to cross the bridge. Halfway across, it stopped for a gun salute. There was a great cheer from the crowd and it then crossed into Cornwall.

Henry stood on tiptoe to try and catch sight of the Prince as he stepped out on to the platform at Saltash, but all he could see were the splendid uniforms of the Prince's bodyguard, and the top of the Prince's hat. All around him he heard words like 'a triumph' and 'the importance of engineering' and 'the science of the future'.

Papa glanced at Henry. 'You hear that?' he said. 'It's quite true. And one day you'll be an engineer too. What better future could you have to look forward to!'

Picture Glossary

Victorian engineers did not just build railways or run factories. They also designed ships, steam engines, farm machinery and huge construction projects such as bridges or viaducts.

On this page you can see drawings of three projects (the Great Western Railway, the S.S. *Great Britain* and the Clifton Suspension Bridge) designed by the most famous engineer of the Victorian period, Isambard Kingdom Brunel. As well as being useful, his designs managed to look good too. Many of them survive today, and can be visited. You will find some in the 'Places to Visit' list on page 30.

S.S. *Great Britain*
Designed by Brunel. When it was launched in Bristol in 1843, it was the largest ship afloat. It is built of iron, and powered by a steam-driven propeller. It can also be powered by sail, and has six masts. In 1970 it was salvaged from the Falkland Islands and towed back to its original dock in Bristol for restoration.

Agricultural machinery
The steam traction engine (right) moved from farm to farm to provide power to drive threshing machines, or, as in this picture, to help with ploughing. The engine would pull the plough to and fro across the field, using a system of wire ropes and pulleys.

One machine could do the work of many horses and men, quickly and cheaply. Farmers saw machines as a way of making more money. Not surprisingly, many farm labourers were afraid that machines would take their jobs. On some farms, there were violent protests and sometimes the new machines were damaged.

In time, the farm-workers were proved right. Machines were used increasingly, to perform a wide variety of agricultural tasks. Many labourers had to move to the towns to work in factories. Engineering had brought 'progress', but it also brought many changes to peoples' lives.

Right: This map shows Henry's journey across the south of England. The Royal Albert Bridge at Saltash opened the railway line from Devon into Cornwall. By 1859 it was possible to travel the 300 miles from London to Truro by train.

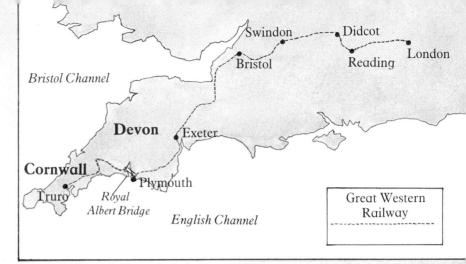

Great Western Railway

Clifton Suspension Bridge

Work began on the bridge in 1836 but soon stopped because of a lack of money. It was finally completed in 1864 as a tribute to Brunel, who had died in 1859. The bridge spans the Avon Gorge at Clifton, near Bristol. It was made of steel, and at 300 metres wide it was the longest suspension bridge in the world.

Finding Out More

Books to Read

The following books contain information about
Victorian engineering:

R. Bowood **Story of the Railways** (Ladybird 1961)

H. Cummings **Early Railways** (Macdonald 1975)

D. & H. Jenkins **Isambard Kingdom Brunel**
  (Wayland 1977)

J. Pudney **Brunel and his World** (Thames and
  Hudson 1974)

W. J. Reader **Life in Victorian England** (Batsford
  1964)

Places to Visit

There are many Victorian buildings and monuments
still standing in Britain, and many working railway
lines, some of them run by local railway preservation
societies. Your local tourist office will be able to give
you details of those that are open to the public. There
are also many museums and heritage centres with
exhibitions (and sometimes demonstrations) of
Victorian engineering:

The Acton Scott Working Farm Museum, Salop

The Beamish North of England Open Air Museum,
  County Durham

The Bradford Industrial Museum

The Bristol Industrial Museum

The British Engineerium, Hove, Brighton

The Great Western Railway Museum, Swindon,
  Wiltshire

The Great Western Railway Society, Didcot,
  Oxfordshire

The Greater Manchester Museum of Science and
  Industry

The Ironbridge Gorge Museum, Telford, Shropshire

Kew Pumping Station, Kew, London

The Museum of Science and History, Birmingham

The National Railway Museum, York

The Nottingham Industrial Museum